DUA LIPA

*

*

*

Flying High to Success

*

*

*

Weird and Interesting Facts on Dua Lipa!

By Bern Bolo

© Bolo Inc. 2017

TABLE OF CONTENTS

***

INTRODUCTION

Hi mate! Nice to see you again. As you have guessed we are back to Trivia Land. It's a new day, new artist, new adventures and new life story that we will uncover. Especially with our artist of the day, she has an interesting life.

Now, I know you're excited but first you need to guess who our artist is. Yes, I know you already know she's a She, do you want more clues or can you guess already? Can you, can you? Ok, ok, you more. Of course, here are the other clues.

Her name meaning in her parents native tongue is "I need it" literally but it could also mean "love" and yes, I use Google translate since her name is so different. With her name being that and thinking her parents homeland, I know it would mean something, so here it is!

The last clue is that before she became a singer she started as a model but her dream and goal in life is to be a musician. I know there might be a few of them but I think since I give out the first name you can guess her right?

With all the clues here, you can guess who it is, right? Anyone? Brownie points and virtual hugs? Oh, come on! No? Alright, alright, I get it.

Our artist of the day is none other than . . . Dua Lipa!

Yes, the sweet face Englishwoman singer is the one we have here! We will uncover all about her, how she got to the top and every little bits that we could find. So sit back and relax. . .

HOW I GET HERE

Dua Lipa was born on 22nd of August 1995 in London. Her parents are Albanian who are native in Pristina, Kosovo. There is no information about her mother but his father is Dukagjin Lipa, a well-known Kosovar Albanian rock singer.

Here a little fact. Did you know that music and dancing is an important part of Albanian culture? Like in weddings, there will be dancing with traditional music played. So, it's natural for the Kosovo London-born singer to be immersed with music at an early age. It's in their blood already!

Ever since Dua was young, she was always listening to her father's songs and her favorite artists like Bob Dylan and Bowie. Personally, her favorite artists were Pink and Nelly Furtado. That's where she got the hip-hop influence and the badass personality, which is fun and she loves being that. Their music, her dad's influence on music and their attitude towards it helped her mold who she wants to be and who she is now.

Of course, there is no such thing as smooth sailing life. Everybody encounters challenges and obstacles in life which is what makes you stronger and more motivated in the long run. Our artist, of course, is no exception to this.

In her primary school days, Dua went to a stage school every weekend. She tried to join the school choir yet she was told that she couldn't sing 'cause she couldn't hit the high notes. I mean, isn't there medium or low notes in a choir? No need to let down the little girl so harshly? And she was really let down when she was told that. Who wouldn't?

Dua admitted that the rejection helps her build her own character, no matter how heartbroken she was. Her parents, apparently, didn't believe the evaluator as well. They brought young Dua to Sylvia Young theater school. There, she gained back here self-confidence but not like a musical performer level, which was good enough for her.

At the age of 14, Dua started posting songs she had covered with on her YouTube channel, cover from the artists like Nelly Furtado, Christina Aguilera and much more. That was the start of her musical career. She gained a lot of attention from it, especially when she started modeling. Dua told all those who she co-work with about them.

Then she made her decision to move back to London and pursue music. Dua was born in London but she and her family moved back to Kosovo last 2008 when they have declared independence and her father's job call for it. It wasn't an easy decision. She was only 15 at that time and she's asking her parent to live apart from them and unsupervised. That's a huge leap of trust (from his parents' side) and independence (from her side).

That was a good thing as well. Being independent early in life makes you think for yourself and consider all your actions before doing them. It gave Dua the maturity but still has merit as an artist.

Fortunately for Dua, she got a permission to go back as long as she still went to school. It was amazing! The independence she feels and the little freedom that she experience was the best. Dua lived with her friends. She went to school every morning and took a job (when she reached the age of 16) as a hostess at nightclub and waitress in restaurants. The darker side of London nightlife and the drama every night became the inspiration for her earlier written songs.

This was the start for her on diving to the self-defined dark pop genre. Making it more uniquely her, she combined it with hip-hop, that gives out a feeling of realness and that its portraying a story. With her husky sultry voice, Dua captured the hearts of everyone who heard her.

She also had a stint in modeling. That ended quickly though when a manager told her that she needs to lose weight if she wants to be successful or want to do the catwalk. Dua mentioned with Billboard that she love food too much to think about dieting and she thinks that her voice is her best asset. I think both are her best assets. Her unique way of dressing herself up still portray her modeling days with her personal touch and her amazing voice as well.

It wasn't long after that, she was found and later signed by Warner Music last 2015 and started working for his debut album.

HERE I AM

Her dreams are starting to come true. All her hard work is coming into fruitions. Dua is releasing songs under the record label of Warner Bros. Record.

Dua revealed that her songs are a combination of pop and hip-hop. The singles were created to make the listeners feel like they are not alone. That there are other people who have the same experience as themselves and for them to know her as well. The audience will be able to take a peak at her life for the past few years.

Her first single "New Love" was released last 21st of August 2015. The producers were Emile Haynie and Andrew Wyatt. The making of the music video for this single was very accidental. They were supposed to shoot another song but it got postponed. So, Dua and a photographer decided to shoot something freestyle. Since it didn't need a massive budget, they went with it and an amazing music video came out!

On the 30th of October 2015 was the releasing of her second single "Be the One". Dua revealed in *BBC* that the "Be the One" wasn't written by her yet it's one of her favorite. When it was aired on Contemporary Hit Radio stations last 30th of December 2016, it got the #9 spot on the UK Single Chart for the first time.

Dua also got a tour named after her single "Hotter Than Hell". The tour is all over UK and Europe started in Ireland to UK, Denmark & Belgium then throughout Germany and ending in Italy, which was last October 2016. It was such a successful tour, sold-out venues, performing unreleased singles, and overall amazing.

She also served an opening act of Troye Sivan's tour called Suburbia Tour last November 2016.

The "Last Dance" was inspired by the feeling of being homesick and upset. Dua was in Toronto for a long time so she poured all her frustrations and emotion to that song. The result was unexpectedly amazing. The single was released last 18th of February 2016

This was quickly followed by "Hotter Than Hell" last 6th of May 2016. The song was all about Dua's relationship on her teenage years. The relationship was toxic and demeaning, where the girl just wants to be wanted and the guy keeps on reminding the girl that she wasn't enough. She altered it a little by having the girl being loved and wanted. She admitted that it help her move on. The single snagged the #15 spot on the UK Single charts while getting the top 20 spot on Australia, Belgium and the Netherlands.

On 26th of August 2016, "Blow Your Mind (Mwah)" was released and immediately snatched the #50 spot of UK Single Chart and continues to rise to #30. The single also snagged the #72 of US Billboard Hot 100, which became the very first single to get in on the said chart, #23 on Billboard Mainstream Top 40 chart and got the top spot on the Billboard Dance Club Songs chart.

Sean Paul's "No Lie" which featured Dua was released last 18th of November 2016 and the collaboration of Martin Garrix and Dua was released last 37th of January 2017 titled "Scared to be Lonely". Dua's latest single "Lost in Your Light" which featured Miguel was released last 21st of April 2017.

All of these songs will be on her self-titled studio album which will be released on, hopefully, the 2nd this June 2017.

We will be expecting more & interesting singles from her in the future. I don't know about you but I enjoy her singles so much! My personal favorites were *Scared to be Lonely, Hotter Than Hell* and *Blow Your Mind (Mwah)*. What about you?

WHAT I GOT

In a short amount of time that she was exposed nationally and internationally, Dua already got the audience hooked to her one of a kind of music. Awards and Nominations came pouring, which was amazing.

Last 2016, she got nominated for the *Sound of...2016* in BBC and the *Best Push Act* in MTV Europe Music Awards. That, however, didn't amount to what she got in 2017.

In the Eurosonic Noorderslag, a four-day music showcase festival in Netherlands, Dua won the *European Border Breakers Awards (EBBA)*, the *Public Choice Award* and the *Best Newcomer of the Year Award*. She also won the NME Awards as the *Best New Artist*.

Dua only got the nomination in NME Awards as the *Best British Female Artist* and in Brit Award as the *Critic's Choice*.

Her singles, on the other hand, got certified to be Platinum of Gold in different countries. Like Dua's "Be The One", it's Gold record in Britain, Germany and Sweden while Platinum record in Australia, Belgium and Italy. That's only the first one.

Her "Hotter Than Hell" got a Gold in Britain and Australia while a Platinum in Sweden and "Blow Your Mind (Mwah)" on the other hand was certified as a Silver record in Britain.

The collaboration with Martin Garrix titled "Scared to be Lonely" was a Silver record in Britain, Gold record in the countries of Belgium and Italy, and Platinum in Australia and Sweden.

This isn't so bad as a new artist right, with those big accomplishment?! Multiple Nomination, a handful of win awards and two or three certified singles. We shall continue to look forward on her upcoming works, so break a leg!

HERE'S SOME LOVE

Love is a very important emotion. It's our greatest strength and our biggest weakness. For our artist, on the other hand, there is nothing we can confirm. It's mostly rumors and when asked she won't give you an answer.

We can understand that though. Artists have most of their life exposed to the public to satisfy their fans. So, if they want some part of their life in private then we shall respect that. It's only a matter of time for us to know who her boyfriend is though. They were seen multiple times together until they just confirmed it.

Later in their relationship, it was confirmed that Dua Lipa's boyfriend was Isaac Carew, a model turned chef. I think that being a chef gives him more points to her since she loves food so much. She might be the food taster every time Isaac cook.

The tight-lipped artist opens her mouth when there was a rumor of that she has a relationship with another. This, another person was Harry Styles, a member of the boy group One Direction. Dua revealed to The Sun that he was just a friend and were just hanging out. Her heart was already captured by a model at the same time a cook.

They look like very much in love for me. So I don't know what happen for them to break up only 18 months with their relationship. They split with no apparent reason yet Dua was said to be moving on. When Isaac was interviewed, he didn't comment on it and Dua is already moving on.

Rumor has it, that Dua was after the heart of another artist. The heart of the artist she's dreaming of having a collaboration with. When she visited the headquarters of Bizarre, Dua revealed, she was going to L.A. to work with a specific person for a specific song and to create a relationship with him.

Now, 'relationship' is too general to know if it's just as a friend or something more. We will found out if they will reveal it or if there will be more sighting. For now, we shall adopt the wait-and-see tactics.

ABOUT ME

There are some little tidbit that you might or might not know about our English pop star. These little things are some not so well-known facts or the reason why people knew Dua will succeed in the music industry.

Well then, let's not waste time and start!

You might not know it but when Dua was in primary school, she took up Cello. She loved it and enjoyed playing it. Unfortunately, she had to give it up since it's becoming quite dangerous to her health. She's just a small child at that time and the cello was really big for her to lugged around. It would hit her head and back repeatedly.

Well, if I was her mother I would do that as well. No matter what the result, it doesn't equate for her health.

At the age of six, Dua had thin hair. Her parents found a solution to thicken it. They shave it off. Yes, you have heard it right. Dua's parents shaved off all of her hair. She loved it, especially when her mom told her she looked like a mini-Demi Moore in the G.I. Jane movie.

I don't know about her but for me, that is so embarrassing! And I'm speaking from experience here! I have the same problem and my parents did the same. Luckily for me, it was when I was young. I have pictures which make it more embarrassing.

Dua's first demo, Lions Tigers and Bears is still on Soundcloud. When asked why it was still there, she answered that she doesn't know herself. It's just her first original work. I think she just wants it there as a remembrance and how she started. A moment you could say.

We all know that at the age of 15, Dua lived on her own right? What you didn't know was she wasn't good in cooking and cleaning, especially doing the laundry. She said in an interview with Nylon that she just put her dirty clothes in a cupboard and bought new ones. Her mother, who would surprise her sometimes, would visit and told her to sort her life. That was the time she seriously started to learn all of it.

We just need a mother's touched to the household chores!

When she started to waiting tables as a part-time job, Dua was able to serve Channing Tatum and his wife once. It was a great time for her; she was able to see his hotness personally. I would love to experience that too!

Her looks and style are as unique as her. You could see her with a choker, leather jacket and fishnets tights most of the time. On an interviewed Dua told Vogue that it was inspired by the Nineties-era. She had a stylist but they have a misunderstanding on what she likes to wear. Sometimes, the stylist will guide her where to buy the stuff she likes in designer shops.

She also told them jokingly that if she wasn't a singer then maybe she's a fairy princess. Dua never has a plan B. That motivated her to work hard and do her best to reach her goal. It's a good way to think, all or nothing kind of thing so you can't afford to fail.

Dua loves to travel and swim and if it's her day off, she admitted that she just want to lie around or sleep. A good plan for a day off!

There may be more of this and we just need to look out! We are happy for your success and looking forward to more of your work!

REFERENCE

https://www.forbes.com/sites/livbuli/2016/03/01/10-reasons-why-dua-lipa-could-become-the-next-big-pop-star/#46c914196f92

https://en.wikipedia.org/wiki/Dua_Lipa

http://www.bbc.co.uk/news/entertainment-arts-35520865

http://www.digitalspy.com/music/new-music/interviews/a776876/meet-your-new-favourite-popstar-dua-lipa-just-dont-call-her-the-new-lana-del-rey/

http://www.billboard.com/articles/columns/pop/7709315/dua-lipa-rejecting-modeling-trove-sivan-strip-club

http://www.bbc.co.uk/programmes/p03br1k6

https://en.wikipedia.org/wiki/Be_the_One_(Dua_Lipa_song)

https://en.wikipedia.org/wiki/Hotter_than_Hell_(Dua_Lipa_song)

https://en.wikipedia.org/wiki/Blow_Your_Mind_(Mwah)

http://www.kosovo-info.com/dua-lipa/

http://www.kosovo-info.com/10-reasons-why-dua-lipa-will-be-successful/

https://www.thesun.co.uk/tvandshowbiz/2723458/dua-lipa-hits-back-at-speculation-she-and-harry-styles-are-in-a-relationship/

https://www.thesun.co.uk/tvandshowbiz/3082384/singer-dua-lipa-sets-eyes-on-calvin-harris-as-she-jets-to-la-to-work-on-future-material/

http://www.nylon.com/articles/dua-lipa-interview

http://www.vogue.co.uk/article/dua-lipa-interview-hotter-than-hell

http://dualipa.com/hotter-hell-tour/

Check Out **SAM HUNT's Trivia!**

Adventure…… I love people like this! Did you know that "Cop Car" is about how he and his ex-girlfriend were caught by cops sneaking into a small airport? Are you updated with an almost spoiled marriage proposal? Do you believe in Fate? How about destiny? Those two joined and you can conquer anything! Our artist of the day had experienced both situations. Did you know that the talent he grew up with wasn't creating music? Our artist of the day's goal in life wasn't originally what he is now. But as you can see, at the age of 33, he is quite famous in his chosen genre. One of the best, actually! Do you know who encourages him to pursue his passion? The person or people he shared his dreams with? The person/people he played some of his songs with and gave him a positive response? The people or person that encourages him to start playing in bars? And…. Now he's one of the best, I'm sure Sam never forget that person/people! Did you know that Our football player, together with a friend, with barely enough amount of supplies, moved to Nashville to follow their dreams and passion? Did you know that he never thought that being a songwriter would be his future job because Football was already ingrained in him and would be hard to forget and let go? Did you know that there was a time in Hunt's life where he almost gave up in country music? All these information and a lot more are inside-- so go ahead and take a peek, and then take one! If you're really into it, take more and give them as gifts to your friends.

Check Out SAM HUNT's Trivia

Get your copy of SAM HUNT's Trivia!

If you enjoyed this "Trivia", please leave an honest review on Amazon.com!

Sign-up here on Bern Bolo's site for Trivia On Twenty One Pilots!